RACE CAR LEGENDS

The Allisons

Mario Andretti

Dale Earnhardt

A. J. Foyt

Richard Petty

The Unsers

CHELSEA HOUSE PUBLISHERS

RACE CAR LEGENDS

A. J. FOYT

Josh Wilker

CHELSEA HOUSE PUBLISHERS
New York Philadelphia

Produced by Daniel Bial and Associates
New York, New York

Picture research by Alan Gottlieb
Cover illustration by Neil Maclachlan

First Printing

1 3 5 7 9 8 6 4 2

Library of Congress Cataloging-in-Publication Data

Wilker, Josh.
    A. J. Foyt / Josh Wilker.
        p.   cm. — (Race car legends)
    Includes bibliographical references and index.
    Summary: A biography of the famous race car driver A. J. Foyt.
    ISBN 0-7910-3178-0 (hc). — ISBN 0-7910-3179-9 (pbk.)
      1. Foyt, A. J., 1935–   —Juvenile literature. 2. Automobile racing
drivers—United States—Biography—Juvenile literature.
[1. Foyt, A. J., 1935–   . 2. Automobile racing drivers.]
I. Title. II. Series   95-8237
GV1032.F66W55   1996   CIP
796.7′2′0922 B—dc20   AC

CONTENTS

THE DRIVE TO WIN

What's the most popular spectator sport in the United States? It's not baseball, football, basketball, or even horse racing. America's favorite sport is automobile racing.

To the outsider, it looks simple. You get in your car, keep the accelerator depressed as you hurtle around the track, expect your crew to keep the car in perfect condition, and try not to go deaf as you weave your machine through traffic toward the checkered flag. But in actuality, it's not at all easy. Just as baseball isn't simply a matter of hitting the ball, so racing is full of subtleties.

What does it take to be a world-class race car driver? The more you know about the lives of the greats, the more it becomes clear that each successful driver is an extraordinary athlete gifted with unusual vision, coordination, and the will to win. The concentration necessary to send a car speeding around a track at 200 miles per hour for hour after hour, when a momentary lapse can cause instant death for him and any unfortunate driver near him, is phenomenal. Any driver worth his salt must be strong, self-confident, resilient, and willing to take risks in order to have an opportunity to win.

In addition, the top drivers have to be good businessmen and know how to put together a winning team. They have to find sponsors to put them in competitive cars. They rely on a pit crew to make sure that their car is always in peak performance condition. And they have to be mentally prepared each race day to take into consideration a host of factors: weather, the other racers, the condition of the track, and how their car is responding on that day. Without everything right, a driver won't stand a chance of winning.

All the drivers in the Race Car Legends series grew up around race cars. The fathers of Richard Petty and Dale Earnhardt were very successful race car drivers themselves. A. J. Foyt's father was a part-time racer and a full-time mechanic; the Allisons and Unsers are an extended family of racers. Only Mario Andretti's father disapproved of his son's racing. Yet Mario and his twin brother Aldo devoted themselves to racing at a young age.

Despite the knowledge and connections a family can provide, few of the legendary racers portrayed in this series met with immediate success. They needed to prove themselves in sprint cars or midget cars before they were allowed to get behind the wheel of a contending stock car or a phenomenally expensive Indy car. They needed to be tested in the tough races on the hardscrabble tracks before they learned enough to handle the race situations at Daytona or the Brickyard. They needed to learn how to get the most out of whatever vehicle they were piloting, including knowing how to fix an engine in the wee hours of the night before a big race.

A driver also has to learn to face adversity, because crashes often take the lives of friends or relatives. Indeed, every driver has been lucky at one point or another to survive a scare or a bad accident. "We've had our tragedies, but what family hasn't?" remarked the mother of Al and Bobby Unser. "I don't blame racing. I love racing as our whole family has."

What each driver has proved is that success in this most grueling sport takes commitment. Walter Payton, the great football running back, and Paul Newman, star of many blockbuster movies, have both taken up racing—and proved they have some talent behind the wheel. Still, it's evident that neither has been able to provide the devotion it takes to be successful at the highest levels.

To be a great driver, racing has to be in your blood.

PLACES NO ONE ELSE WILL GO

All the other drivers stopped and stared as the kid walked by. They knew him. He was Tony Foyt's son. They'd seen him hanging around race tracks with his father the mechanic since he was a little boy. They had never seen him like this. He was here to race.

Unlike the other drivers in their grease-stained t-shirts and jeans, Tony Foyt's son wore spotless white pants and a blazing red shirt made of silk. The pit area at Houston Playland Park that night in 1953 buzzed with talk about the new driver in the gaudy outfit. Most rookies would have shied away from any extra attention. The lean, handsome eighteen-year-old was not like other rookies. Anthony Joseph Foyt, Jr., already had a motto by then: "If you're going to do something, do it big."

He wheeled his midget race car onto the track. A. J. knew the car was fast. At Tony Foyt's auto repair shop, father and son had worked togeth-

Tony Foyt (right) was a mechanic and taught his son A. J. (left) all he knew about going fast.

9

er for many days to turn the car into a formidable racing machine. Sometimes, if there was more work to be done, the younger Foyt labored all night long under the glare of the auto shop lights.

He knew the car so well, in fact, that as he blasted around the dirt track, attempting to qualify for the first race of the night, he sensed something was wrong. After the qualifying run, Foyt complained to his father about the car's lack of power, ignoring a wild cheer that was ripping through the crowd. Tony Foyt told his son to relax. He had just broken the Playland Park track record of Indianapolis 500 champion Johnnie Parsons.

He had broken the track record despite the fact that his engine had been doctored. Tony Foyt, concerned that his excited son would try to go too fast in his new midget racer, had sapped power from the engine by retarding the magneto. It was as if a sprinter had broken the record for the 100-yard dash while wearing lead weights attached to his ankles.

The elder Foyt, who had been around racing all his life, knew enough about the sport to be concerned for his son. He had seen men crippled in explosive, flame-riddled crashes. He had seen men killed. A. J. knew the risks, too. Spending his whole life around race tracks had taught him that "the limp, and the fact that they all were a little broke, was the way you could tell race drivers from the rest of society."

Tony Foyt and his friend Jimmy Greer watched from the pits as A. J. took his place at the starting line for the first race of the night. To give A. J. a car to race in, the two men had scraped together every spare penny they had. They had scram-

PLACES NO ONE
ELSE WILL GO

11

bled to work every angle, finding a deal on a Kur-
tis-Kraft chassis and buying the Offenhauser
engine from the widow of a driver who had died
in a crash. They had gone without all luxuries.
Greer and his family ate off a picnic table in a
house with old sheets on the windows. Prior to
the big night of racing, Greer's wife had told A.
J. that he better start winning quickly. "I'm not
going to eat off a damn picnic table the rest of
my life," she said.

If the first race was any indication, Mrs. Greer
would have her dining room table soon enough.
A. J. shot into the lead in the second lap of the
four-lap dash and held on to win. He won the
second race, too, broadsliding through the tricky
turns of the quarter-mile oval like an old pro.
By the beginning of the third race, fans crowd-
ing the fence at trackside were covered with dirt
thrown from all the race cars' wheels. By the end
of that race they were muddier than ever and
reeling with joyous disbelief. The kid had won
again.

He took his place at the back of the pack to
start the fourth and final race. Due to an invert-
ed start—the fastest cars last and the slowest
cars first—A. J. would have to pass every driver on the track to win. Many of the drivers had
been manhandling race cars around the dirt
track at Playland Park for years. They knew all
the tricks, and they weren't afraid to use them.
Completing the volatile mix of drivers now deter-
mined to beat the rookie were a number of reckless amateurs whose abandon far outstripped
their skill.

A dirt-track race at Playland Park in 1953, like
other dirt races of the time, constantly teetered
on the brink of disaster. Winning was mostly a

It's not hard to get boxed in when you're driving in midget car races, as A. J. Foyt discovers here.

by-product of survival. Ruts and oil slicks laced a track surrounded only by a flimsy fence. The cockpits of the cars had no protective cages made of roll bars and the drivers did not wear fireproof suits. Drivers took a beating as they muscled their ill-handling cars over the bumpy track. Rocks and stray shards of metal on the track flew up into the open cockpits.

Foyt later recalled, "In some ways, the early days are the most dangerous. You run races that aren't real fast, but you run 'em as hard as you can. The tracks aren't real good, the cars aren't real good, and a lot of the drivers aren't real good." Just to finish all four races on his first day in his new car would have been an accomplishment for a teen-aged driver. But A. J. wanted more than that.

It was clear to all who were watching that he was capable of much more than mere survival on the track. The way he bulled the car through the turns, sending high rooster tails of dirt to the sky, set him apart from the other drivers. Not long after the races at Playland Park that night, a mechanic named Cecil Taylor remarked, "Watching Foyt on dirt was like watching a concert. Artistry in motion. It was a beautiful thing to watch. He'd be running fast and be sitting back in the car like in a rocking chair, all relaxed and everything under control, with those clods flying up. Those were men who drove those cars in those days; they weren't boys. And A. J., he was the Man."

The drivers gunned their engines, waiting for the race to start. In their rearview mirrors they all caught a glimpse of blazing red in the cockpit of the last car in the line. A. J., still wrapped in his regal silk shirt, fastened his helmet and slipped his goggles into place. Jimmy Greer leaned over and mouthed a common racing phrase. It is meant to encourage the racer to throw fear our the window and pump the throttle with everything they've got. Jimmy Greer said to A. J., "Stand on it."

A. J. left four cars in the dust by the first turn. By the second turn, half the cars in the race were receding in his rearview mirror. He avoided two spinning cars by shooting low onto the grass and hurtled back onto the track to continue his climb. He drove deeper and deeper into every corner, skidding within inches of the fence, grazing other cars as he slipped by. It didn't seem possible that he could be driving like he was and still be under control. Within a few laps he had passed all but one of the drivers.

A crafty veteran named Buddy Rackley guarded his lead. He ranged high and low to block the charging rookie. A. J. could not get past. Rackley hogged the inside in the second-to-last turn on the last lap and Foyt broke high. He edged forward through a sliver of daylight on the back straightaway and they sailed toward the final turn dead even. In the turn Rackley still held the inside. In an attempt to make the rookie back off, Rackley veered high, forcing Foyt toward the outer wall.

The race had whittled down to a single choice. Foyt could ease off the accelerator and settle for second-place money. Or he could attempt to gun it through a narrow opening and risk running his wheels over Rackley's—a sure way to catapult into a ferocious crash.

Automobile racers know that taking risks can be thrilling. Racing great Tony Bettenhausen once said, "Some guys are dead without knowing it. They don't appreciate life. Risking it makes us feel alive."

Two-time Indianapolis 500 champion Rodger Ward traced the line that connects risk-taking with winning when he said, "I will put myself in places on a race that most drivers will not go." It was in the mid-sixties when Ward said that, a decade after A. J. Foyt's debut at Playland Park. Ward had passed on the mantle of the United States Auto Club (USAC) national championship to a young charger from Houston, Texas. He paid tribute to his successor by saying, "Foyt is the greatest of drivers because he will put himself in places no one else will go."

"I could never settle for being anything but the best," Foyt said. "I've always loved racing more than anything in my life and if I couldn't be the best at it, my life wouldn't mean much to me."

As Rackley pushed him toward the wall, A. J. Foyt heard a voice in his head. It said, "Stand on it." He hammered the throttle to the floor and the checkered flag sprung to life for him and him alone.

"I GUESS YOU'RE GONNA BE A RACE DRIVER"

Soon after Anthony Joseph Foyt, Jr., was born, on January 16, 1935, in Houston, Texas, he was following his father to work. "When I was a little bitty kid," said A. J., "I'd do anything just to be with him." A. J. came to love the gasoline-laced air of the B and F garage.

B and F stood for Burt and Foyt, partners in business and also a local racing team. Dale Burt drove and Tony Foyt was the mechanic. A love of cars and of racing ran in the Foyt blood. Tony's father had also been a mechanic. Tony himself had driven race cars. "I never won none of my races," he said. "We run for nothin'. We were more or less just having a bunch of fun."

At the garage, Tony Foyt used to place his son on a high metal stool in an attempt to keep the toddler from getting in the way. A. J. soon wriggled down from the high perch, eager to get closer to the action. He peppered his father with questions as the mechanic worked on an engine.

A. J. at age three. His dad said, "I bought my boy a toy racer just for fun, but he really took to it."

His first questions about the world always seemed to concern the same subject. "That's all he had interest in—cars," said his father.

A. J. started driving not too long after he had learned how to walk. For his third birthday, he received a go cart built by his father. A. J. spent hour after hour bombing around the outside of the house, imitating the drivers at the Houston race tracks. Like the drivers he got to see as the youngest member of the B and F racing team, A. J. found he could pick up speed if he started his slide into the corners early. Two years later, when A. J. was five, his father built him his own midget racer.

"I thought that little old car was the most beautiful thing there ever was," said A. J. about the blue and white car.

"It could go 50 miles an hour," Tony remembered, "and he would go 50 in it." A. J. got so good at flying around the yard in the midget that one night his dad set up a pre-race exhibition at the Houston Speed Bowl.

A. J. was only expected to take a lap around the track by himself, but he didn't see much point in that. So he swaggered up to one of the best racers in Houston, a man named Doc Cossey, and said, "Doc, I can outrun that midget of yours." Cossey started chuckling and didn't stop until he was chewing on the dust of the five-

He was only five years old and his midget car had only three horsepower. Still, the amazingly precocious Foyt beat veteran driver Doc Cossey.

year-old's quick start as the green flag dropped. A. J. whipped the car around the track like a seasoned veteran and won the race. "I guess it was then and there," A. J. later reflected, "I knew I wanted to be a race car driver."

A. J. longed to get behind the wheel of the real thing, one of the two B and F midget racers. When he was 11 years old, his parents went to Dallas to race one of their cars and left A. J. behind to babysit his little sister Marlene. He sensed it was his big chance. With the help of three friends, he wheeled the racer that had been left behind out of the garage and he got it started. A. J. sent his friends into a whooping, hollering frenzy by blasting around the outside of his house at full throttle, lap after lap, faster each time. Then they were all shook by a loud explosion. The engine burst into flames.

Tony and Evelyn came home later that night. "The grass was chewed to pieces and there were tire gouges all around," Tony said. "The swings in the yard had been knocked down. I went into the house and right into his bedroom. He played like he was asleep, but he wasn't. I could tell."

A. J. was well aware that his father was a stern disciplinarian, and he was bracing himself for the worst. From the other room came his mother's voice, "Don't say anything to him right now when you're so mad."

By the next morning, Tony Foyt had come to realize exactly what the incident meant. It wasn't that A. J. was out to disobey him. It was more that A. J. had something inside him, like a hunger. It needed feeding. When his son emerged from his room the next morning, Tony Foyt calmly said, "I guess you're gonna be a race driver, A. J."

By the time A. J. was halfway through his senior year of high school, he decided that he needed to chase his dream full time. "I couldn't study any more. I just couldn't wait any longer." He dropped out of school and started racing. His first races were in a 14-year-old stock car that he had bought for $100. At the same time, he was sneaking his father's midget racer out to a local racetrack to run full-speed laps in the dark.

At first, his father refused to consider making A. J. a part of his racing team. A. J. got a ride racing a banged-up midget car for a man named Red Fondren. "If a car doesn't handle," Foyt said about his first midget car, "you make it handle." By the time he was 18, A. J. started turning some heads with his ability to strong-arm a lesser car to the front of the pack.

One of those watching closely was A. J., Sr. He did not enjoy watching his son careen dangerously around a dirt track in Fondren's rattling bucket of bolts. He told A. J., "You gotta get something better under you or quit."

"This thing has gone too far!" screeched A. J.'s worried mother upon learning of Houston's newest racing partnership. "She didn't want me to drive race cars," said A. J. "But she stood behind me when I decided to do it. And she told me how good I was. She gave me some pride in what I was doing. She always encouraged me. 'You're as good as anybody else,' she said."

Foyt quickly started proving her right. After beating Buddy Rackley to sweep the card at Houston Playland Park, Foyt ranged to tracks all over the Southwest to display an overpowering hunger for the checkered flag. Word spread fast among the other drivers: The kid in the silk shirt will beat you any way he can. "You had to be a little wild," said Foyt, "if you were going to be a winner."

He didn't mind backing up his brash racing tactics with his fists. His lifelong reputation as a hot-tempered brawler was born on the steamy dirt tracks of Texas, Oklahoma, and Louisiana. "I drove hard and rough, and that in itself tends to cause tempers to get out of hand," Foyt said. "But the complaint office was always open in my pit." Everyone learned to stay clear of a the volatile racing phenom, especially after a loss. "Getting too close to A. J. when things is going bad," said his father, "is about like trying to dance with a chainsaw."

The elder Foyt kept the wild racer in line. Once, during practice laps, A. J. was goofing around and Tony told his son to stop it. When A. J. ignored his command, he tackled him. With the help of another man, he kept A. J. pinned to the ground until the race started.

There was no harsher punishment than not allowing Foyt to race. Driving a midget car on a dirt track made Foyt feel ten feet tall. "It's like you are overriding some basic law of physics. Your left-front wheel is off the ground and you're sliding through a turn on three wheels. If you have time to look up in the rearview mirror, you can see a roostertail of dirt kicking up behind you, and I'll tell you, you are in heaven."

"Anything he puts his mind to he makes a go of," Tony Foyt once said (shown here tuning up a car while A. J. looks on). "I'll tell you, he's pretty dang hard to beat."

3

"THE KID CAN CUT IT"

In the 1950s, the long trail to the Indianapolis 500 led through the dangerous sprint-car circuit. If a driver proved himself in a sprint car, he might just impress an Indy Car owner enough to get a ride in the legendary race. A. J. Foyt started racing sprint cars in 1955, which he called "the most ferocious race cars you can find." He quickly realized why many drivers considered sprint car racing the highest of challenges. He said, "Some of the hardest races I ever had—been so tired and beat up with blood running out of my eye and all—have been sprint races on the dirt. Got out of there many a time and there'd be just solid blood on my shoulder and around my face. They'd run those big old knobby tires, and they just dug and threw stones and dirt, just like a guy shot you with a shotgun."

Foyt proved he could handle a sprint car and in 1957 was invited to join Wally Meskowski's

Dean Van Lines was Foyt's ticket to the Indianapolis 500. Here Foyt pilots Dean's car in a 1958 race in Phoenix, Arizona.

renowned racing team. It seemed to Foyt that a crack at the Indy 500 wasn't far away. He ran over 50 races that year, nearly a race per week, and he ran them all with reckless abandon. He wanted to get to the top and he didn't care too much about the risks. "I drove every race like it was my last one," he said.

One man who took notice was the reigning USAC champion, a hard-charging driver named Jimmy Bryan. Bryan recommended Foyt to Bryan's boss, Indy Car owner Al Dean. It didn't take long for Dean to pass judgment on the young driver. Early in 1958 Dean proclaimed, "The kid can cut it." With that, A. J. Foyt finally had his ride for the Indianapolis 500.

When Foyt first arrived at the Speedway to begin the month-long preparations for the race, he was overwhelmed. First of all, the sheer size of the place awed him. The grandstands could hold over a quarter of a million people and the track itself was five times bigger than any track he had ever raced on. He was also awed by the imposing history of the place. Some of the greatest triumphs in all of racing had occurred at the Speedway, and some of the greatest racers had built their legends there. As Foyt considered the names of racing greats like Wilbur Shaw, Mauri Rose, and Louie Meyer, he wondered if he could take his place among them. Briefly, he wondered if he belonged at the track at all.

This doubt faded as soon as Foyt got behind the wheel. A veteran named Pat O'Connor gave the rookie some basic tips and then led Foyt around the track for a few laps. Foyt soon found his own best path around the track—what the racers call "the groove." He qualified for twelfth position, the highest of any rookie driver.

Foyt was close enough to the front to witness a deadly first-lap crash involving close to half of the 33 cars in the race. The two front runners, Ed Elisian and Dick Rathmann, tangled in turn three, causing the third-place driver, Jimmy Reece, to slow up, and Bob Veith hit Reece. Pat O'Connor's car hit Reece's and flew 50 feet, exploding into flames on impact with the ground. The disastrous chain reaction continued as Jerry Unser's car flipped up and over a wall and more than a dozen cars reeled and spun. Foyt muscled his car into a slide to slow it down and slipped through a narrow opening between two cars to escape the crash unharmed.

Pat O'Connor showed Foyt some of the ropes at the Indianapolis 500. But in the very first lap of Foyt's first race, a crash claimed O'Connor's life.

The yellow caution flag slowed the race to a crawl for 20 laps as track workers cleared the wreckage. Foyt stole a glance at Pat O'Connor's flame-blackened car and knew instantly that the man who had showed him around the track was dead. For the rest of the race, Foyt drove as if enveloped by fog. "The spirit wasn't there," said Foyt. For the first time in his life, he drove tentatively. His race ended on lap 148, when the car skidded in water from a broken hose, traveling 1,000 feet backward before hitting a wall.

Foyt said his goodbyes to Pat O'Connor and to Indy, but before he left he vowed that he would be back. He would be tougher and harder, and there would only be one thing on his mind: winning. "I would never get close to a race driver again," Foyt said.

In the 1959 Indy 500, Foyt charged from his starting position in the middle of the pack to get as close as fifth by the time the race was half over. Had he not been bumped into a long slide by Duane Carter, he might have continued his climb. As it was, the car was not the same after the collision, and he came in tenth. "Close isn't enough," an inconsolable Foyt grumbled after the race. "You win or you lose. I can win, but I don't think the car can."

Foyt's dissatisfaction with Al Dean's racing team, and with Dean's mechanic Clint Brawner in particular, grew as the year went on. He won three USAC races, but he was sure he could have won more. At the end of the season he broke with Dean to race for Bob Bowes, whose mechanic, George Bignotti, was building a reputation not unlike Foyt's own. Racer Bobby Unser described Bignotti accurately when he said, "He's a competitor who'll walk over people to win races, who'll take the gold out of their teeth if he has to."

Foyt's relationship with Bignotti was stormy from the start. The two ultra-competitive men bickered constantly. After another disappointing finish at Indy in 1960, Foyt declared to his wife, Lucy, whom he had married five years earlier, "I'm no better off than I was with Clint Brawner." Foyt threatened to quit racing. Lucy convinced him to try one more race. It was sound advice.

Foyt started to win. He pushed Bignotti to the breaking point. The mechanic admitted, "Before I finished my first season with Foyt I needed pills to calm my nerves." But the team was nearly impossible to beat. Going into a late season race in Phoenix, Arizona, Foyt only needed to finish in the middle of the pack to snare the USAC crown away from reigning champion Rodger Ward. Foyt stood on it from start to finish, lapping the entire field, Ward included, taking his victory lap at full throttle, and sending a triumphant curtain of dirt skyward as he slid sideways into the victory circle.

The streaking racer set his sights on Indianapolis. About the legendary race he said, "It's more people and more money than a man could dream of, the fastest cars and the best drivers anywhere, dangerous as it could be and so damned nervy and exciting it sort of sends a shiver through you. You race wherever you can, whenever you can, but May at Indianapolis is what matters most."

In 1961, a flamboyant braggart named Eddie Sachs snagged pole position for America's biggest race. Sachs, known as The Clown Prince of Racing, loved to put on a show for the fans at Indy. One year he had brought in his own jazz band to play concerts from the infield. Another year, the spirit moved him to jump into the pre-race parade to wave at the crowd with an imaginary baton.

Foyt started the race from the seventh position. He did not make as much noise about winning as the boastful Sachs in the days leading up to the race. But that didn't mean he wasn't supremely confident. On the day of the race, he motioned to the pace car that was always given to the winner of the 500 and vowed to his mother, "I'm gonna win that car."

4

A TOUGH CHAMPION

The 1961 Indianapolis 500 featured spectacular racing from the start. Jim Hurtubise blasted in front in the first lap. The young driver, who had earlier capped a blazing qualifying run by proclaiming about the hallowed Brickyard, "It ain't so tough," held first for 35 laps.

When his engine went sour, Rufus Parnell Jones (better known as Parnelli Jones) took over. A chunk of loose debris from an earlier wreck kicked up and struck Jones in the forehead. He kept his car in front as blood gushed down into his goggles. "It was like I was looking through a glass of tomato juice," quipped Parnelli Jones.

Jones, in first for 75 miles, dropped back eventually with mechanical troubles. Eddie Sachs claimed the lead, carrying with him a shadow named A. J. Foyt. Foyt feinted up high, testing the new front-runner. He knew he would have

At the 1961 Indy 500, A. J. Foyt (#1) led Eddie Sachs (#12) most of the way. Sachs took the lead with 11 laps remaining, but Foyt regained it with only three to go.

Foyt celebrates his 1961 victory at the Indy 500. "It was a tough era in racing," Foyt said later. "So I felt it needed a tough champion."

his work cut out for him. "I had always marveled," said Foyt of Sachs, "at how he could handle a car. It's why he was so hard to get past."

Foyt gambled and shot as low as he could go on a turn, almost catching the grassy infield that would have sent him spinning. He managed to squeeze past Sachs, but Sachs jumped back in front in the straightaway. "There was no question that his car was faster than mine," Foyt said, "so I knew I would have to outdrive him in the corners."

Time and again, Foyt found narrow openings, up high and down low, to sneak past Sachs in the corners, only to see his lead turn to dust in the straights. They traded first place 10 times as the race wore on. Lucy Foyt spoke for the electrified crowd when she later recalled, "It was like it was hard to breathe."

The drivers locked in the duel both began to wonder if they and their cars could hold up under the strain. "There was no margin for error, no room for mistake," Sachs said. "It was a matter of which one of us would break first." Foyt, for his part, had the utmost faith in Bignotti's ability to build him a car that would last the entire race. He was not immune to the pressure, however, admitting, "Your nerves cause you to sort of hallucinate at times."

Both men made pit stops with 30 miles to go for what they hoped would be the final time. Coming back out onto the track, Foyt could sense something different about his car. As if it had somehow shucked off weight, the car felt faster. He blasted by Sachs and started building a lead. Foyt could almost taste the victory when a pit member flashed him a sign that read, "Fuel low." A fuel line had clogged on the last pit stop. The lighter fuel tank had given Foyt extra speed, but it also would apparently cost him the race. He had to pull into the pit again as Sachs sped on toward an apparent win.

There seemed to be no way now for Foyt to triumph, but still he pushed on desperately, not allowing Sachs to ease up. His dogged pursuit paid off. With only five laps left, the white warning layer appeared on Sachs's right rear tire. "At the speeds Eddie was running trying to stay ahead," said Foyt, "he had worn through the tread rubber." Sachs could either pit for new tires and lose the race or hope the tire held up. If it held, he would win. If it didn't, he would crash. It was the type of decision Foyt himself had been faced with many times, going back to his battle with Buddy Rackley in Houston. Foyt always risked the worst for a chance at winning.

Sachs headed for a visit with his pit crew. "I'd rather finish second than finish dead," he said.

Foyt accelerated into the lead, this time for good. Most anyone, had they been in Sachs's position, would have done as he had done. Foyt was different. After winning his first Indianapolis 500 he gave credit to Sachs but confided that if their roles had been reversed, as he said, "I'd have gone on." He realized this set him apart from other racers. "Everyone wants to win," he observed, "but not everyone is willing to make the sacrifices it takes."

Foyt took the checkered flag at 18 other USAC races that year to win his second straight national championship. He became the youngest driver ever to win both Indy and the national championship in the same year. Such an honor wasn't enough to make him rest on his laurels. "You can't really relax or you fall behind. Mother told me years ago that when you get to the top there is only one way to go, and that's down. It takes hard work to be king of the hill and harder work to stay on top."

No one worked harder than Foyt. Long-time racing team crew chief Ray Nichels said of him,

A. J. Foyt often fought with George Bignotti (left), but the mechanic was by his side for many of Foyt's major victories.

"He'll try anything and he'll go from sunup to sundown to get the job done. If it's not finished then, he'll work around the clock." His constant striving for perfection eventually put him at odds with his mechanic. George Bignotti wearied of Foyt's constant second-guessing. "A. J. is not the easiest guy to get along with," he said. Foyt was able to admit years later that "our problem was that George was an absolute genius on engines and I knew enough to bother him."

The feud between the two reached a breaking point at the 1962 Indianapolis 500. Failing brakes caused Foyt to fall out of the lead, and, a few laps later, the left rear wheel flew off, ending his race. The mechanical failures made the toppled champion rage. "The only man in the crew I can trust is my father," A. J. fumed. Bignotti and Foyt parted ways soon after.

Neither man was able to find much success the rest of the year. Rodger Ward springboarded from his second Indy 500 win to grab the USAC national championship. Ward found fault with his rival's hard-charging style by saying, "He runs too hard, too often, and takes too much out of his equipment." Ward wasn't the only one taking aim at Foyt. A. J. bitterly noted, "Everyone wants to beat Foyt. It gives the boys a big laugh."

Foyt realized that the only way he would be able to turn back all his challengers would be to reunite with Bignotti. He also took some of Ward's criticism to heart. "I used to think I carried my cars across. Now I know better. I know they carry me."

Foyt completed all 12 Indy Car races he entered in 1963. "I know now that to finish first I have to finish," said the man who finished first enough times to reclaim the USAC championship. Foyt also began to make his mark as a driver who could win in any kind of car and on any kind of track by cruising to victory in two sports-car road races in Nassau, the Bahamas.

Foyt also spent time that year testing tires at the Indianapolis Speedway for Goodyear Tires. Foyt's keen feel for a race car helped Goodyear eventually develop tires that outperformed those of longtime Indy 500 tire kingpin Firestone. His long hours of testing at the Speedway did more than just help Goodyear tires. "The thousands of miles I put in at Indy didn't hurt me, either," he said. "I know this old track pretty good now. It's a very tricky track. It takes a lot of practice and the only place you can practice for this place is right here."

In 1964, it seemed at first that Foyt's intimate knowledge of the Speedway would not be enough to win. In the month leading up to the race, all the talk among race fans was about the revolutionary rear-engine cars. Two years earlier, some European drivers and an American racer and Europhile named Dan Gurney started to bring them onto the track. At first they couldn't compete with the conventional front-engine roadsters. By 1964, however, it was clear that the rear-engine cars were faster.

A skeptical A. J. Foyt sounded an alarm about the rear-engine cars to anyone who would listen. "These new cars just seem like a bunch of sticks strung together with chicken wire," he said. "Instead of tucking the tanks away from you, there are fuel tanks all around the cockpit and they're full of gasoline, which is a lot more explosive than alcohol. They surround you with

stuff that can blow you to kingdom come in a second."

Most of the top racers chose to ignore Foyt's warning. Eddie Sachs, growing desperate for a win at Indy, spoke for many drivers when he said, "We'll lose to 'em if we don't take our chances with 'em."

Foyt was never averse to taking a chance if it meant getting a shot at victory. But he figured he had that shot already. As Bignotti said, referring to the European racers, "The Grand Prix guys simply know more about these cars than we do. But we know more about this race than they do." To take a chance in the dangerous new cars, Foyt figured, would be like playing Russian roulette.

In lap number 2 of the 500, a rookie driver named Dave MacDonald lost control of his rear-engine car. MacDonald hit a bump in the track

Johnny Rutherford (left, #86) and Ronnie Duman (#64) survived this crash at the 1964 Indianapolis 500. Eddie Sachs, the Clown Prince of Racing, and Dave McDonald were in the middle of the crash. They did not survive.

in turn 4 and smacked first the inner wall and then, spinning wildly, the car aflame, crashed against the outer wall. Eddie Sachs, trailing Mac-Donald tightly, was helpless. His car speared MacDonald's and then exploded on impact with the wall. Foyt came out of turn 2 on the opposite side of the track to see cars spinning and sliding in every direction and twin columns of thick black smoke rising from the cars of Sachs and MacDonald. Foyt said, "It looked like an atomic bomb had dropped."

The Indianapolis 500 came to a stop. Only once before had the race been halted, and that time had been for rain. In the 105 minutes it took for workers to clean up the track, A. J. Foyt did not allow himself to think about what nearly everyone at the Speedway knew: both men were goners. Eddie Sachs had died immediately and Dave MacDonald would die a few hours later in a hospital bed. A. J. said, "That wasn't the time to know. I knew, but I didn't want to know. I knew I had to go on."

Soon after, the race resumed and Foyt took over. His relentless competitive spirit steeled him against the haunting image of the crash. He methodically built an insurmountable lead. As other racers allowed thoughts of the crash to slip into their minds, Foyt pressed on. Even the great Rodger Ward admitted, "I made mistakes. I was shaken by what happened. I was seeing ghosts, I guess." Ward, in second, dropped farther and farther behind.

Foyt pressed on, hungry for speed and victory. He lapped the entire field, winning in record time.

In a somber Victory Lane, Foyt finally let the bad news sink in. He couldn't speak for a few moments. Then he managed to utter, "I'm sorry. I'm sorry those guys died. They were my friends." A. J. paid tribute to MacDonald and said Sachs "had more guts than any of us."

Soot and grime covered his face; his lips were raw and cracked. His rumpled, dirty racing suit had been blown wide open at the elbow during the race. "You got to carry on," he said. "You can't let anyone get too close to you in this game. If they get killed, it breaks your heart. And if you're going to race," A. J. Foyt concluded, "you've got to race alone."

5

"I WENT FLYING"

DEALERS

Parnelli Jones's 1964 Indy 500 had ended in terrifying fashion: Flames from a gasoline fire engulfed his body. But he was soon back behind the wheel, racing. Jim Hurtubise crashed in a race just after Indy that year and doctors told him that his mangled hand would have to be set in one permanent position. He told them to mold it so he could grip a steering wheel. "If you're a racer," said A. J. Foyt after the tragic crash at Indianapolis in 1964, "you go on."

Foyt grabbed his first National Association for Stock Car Auto Racing (NASCAR) win on July 4th in Daytona by outdueling stock car great Bobby Isaac in the last lap. At an Indy Car race at Langhorne, Pennsylvania, the temperature soared to 132 degrees and Foyt's power steering failed, but Foyt just cranked a little harder on the wheel and won. In Trenton, New Jersey,

Foyt followed up his 1964 Indy win with many victories behind the the wheel of a stock car. Here he competes in a USAC 200-mile race at Hanford, California.

the track temperature reached 140 degrees. Rodger Ward led before collapsing in the pits. Jim McElreath took over until he too wilted in the heat. "Was it hot out there?" asked an unstoppable Foyt in victory lane. "I'll have to ask some of the boys about that."

Foyt set a record for most consecutive Indy Car wins—seven—by holding off Bobby Marshman at Springfield by less than a second. His ninth win, at the Indianapolis Fairgrounds, set the record for most Indy Cars wins in a season, and gave him 25 Indy Car victories in his career, another record. He celebrated by roaring past Parnelli Jones at Sacramento for win number 26.

Win number 27 was a little harder to come by. In January 1965, on his way to a stock car race in Riverside, California, Foyt was struck by a gloomy premonition. "I called Lucy and told her where I'd parked the car and where to find the keys. That's something I'd never done before."

Foyt's brakes failed just as he was making a move in the second turn of the Riverside road course to burst past Junior Johnson and Marvin Panch. Foyt had a choice: plow Marvin Panch into the upper wall and stay on the track, or jerk the car off the course and pray. "If you've gotta go," said Foyt, "you do your damnedest not to take anyone with you."

One of Foyt's front wheels caught in a hole in the dirt as he careened off the track. Foyt shot off a 35-foot embankment and flew 50 feet, slipping end over end, finally crashing bottom-side up in a thunder of crumpling metal and kicked-up sand and mud. The first doctor to approach the scene shouted back to the other rescue workers, "Don't hurry. He's dead."

Parnelli Jones rushed past that doctor and clambered into the wreckage to clear the dirt from his suffocating rival's mouth. Foyt wasn't dead, but he was banged up worse than he ever had been before. He had a bad concussion, a broken back, a crushed sternum, a broken left heel, cuts and torn flesh on his face and hands and, as he added, "My whole body was a mass of bruises." He regained consciousness a day after the crash to phone his mother and tell her he was all right and then passed out again for another day.

Foyt refused to abide by his doctor's belief that he would never be able to race again. By swimming daily and taking long walks, Foyt was ready to get back to racing after only three months. At the track in Phoenix, Foyt had to use a cane to get around and constant jolts of pain shot up his back. Instead of screaming in agony, which is what he later admitted he wanted to do, Foyt joked with the other racers about the crash and then went out and won the pole position. Television commentator and magazine editor Chris Economaki remarked, "It was one of the most incredible comebacks any man has ever made."

At an Atlanta, Georgia, stock car race a week later Foyt's vision began to blur from the pain in his back. He kept the car in the race until the throttle got stuck wide open and, as Foyt put it, "I went flying high, wide, and handsome." Foyt escaped this crash unscathed. In fact, when teammate Marvin Panch collapsed from heat exhaustion, Foyt took over and drove Panch's car to victory.

"If you can't beat 'em, join 'em," he said. Foyt, as he had proclaimed earlier, raced alone. But when the time came to help another driver he did not turn away. His split-second decision at Riverside, which may have saved Panch's life, proved that. On a less dramatic note, Foyt often helped young drivers get started. Even in 1965, when Foyt was struggling more than he had in years, he went out of his way to aid a fledgling driver named Bobby Unser. At one race, Foyt loaned Unser tires and set the chassis up and did, as Unser said, "everything but drive it for me."

Foyt, in a dirt car, leads against rear-engine Indy cars at a Milwaukee race in 1965. (Dan Gurney and Mario Andretti are directly behind A. J.) Said Johnny Rutherford of Foyt's performance, "That was unheard of."

Foyt gave Bobby's brother Al an even greater break that year at Indy by offering the rookie a ride in his backup car. "I've often wondered why the man did a thing like that," said Al Unser. "It has meant a lot to me over the years. I wasn't anything, and there were experienced drivers standing in line to get in that backup car." Stock car legend Richard Petty described the two sides of A. J. Foyt by saying, "Away from a race car...he'll do anything in the world for you. But you put him in a car and, man, he's a holy terror."

Foyt labored through mishap after mishap in 1965. "Maybe it's time to quit," mused Foyt after the gearbox in his racer gave way in the 300th mile of the Indy 500. "Everything has gone wrong for me this year." No matter how wrong things went, however, and no matter what he said to the contrary, Foyt refused to quit.

He arrived at a race on pavement in Milwaukee, Wisconsin, to find that his dirt car had mistakenly been shipped there. Any other racer would have surmised that a dirt car would have no chance on pavement against cars designed specifically for that surface. Foyt announced to his crew, "Men, we came here to race and this little car is all we've got. Let's get unloaded and go to work." He outdrove all his rivals to earn the pole position and only a blistered right rear tire late in the race kept him from winning. He finished second.

Second wasn't good enough. Foyt began to look for reasons for his string of bad luck. George Bignotti could sense what was coming. "When the car falls out," said the mechanic, "naturally I get the blame." After the engine overheated at a race in Langhorne, Pennsylvania, in 1965, Foyt announced, "I was going to give up racing, but I decided to give up my mechanic instead." Bignotti seemed almost relieved that his tumultuous union with Foyt had finally been severed. "He's not an easy man to beat," Bignotti said, "but maybe it'll be easier to beat him than live with him."

Bignotti's replacement, Johnny Pouelson, didn't last long. Before a race in 1966 Foyt's crew was working through the night to correct a problem with his car. Pouelson wanted to take a break for dinner and Foyt refused, saying, "We're gonna stay right here until we get this thing straightened out." Pouelson went out for a sandwich and returned only to say, "I quit."

It seemed that no one could keep pace with Foyt. As he tried to regain the form that had brought him to the top, he worked harder than

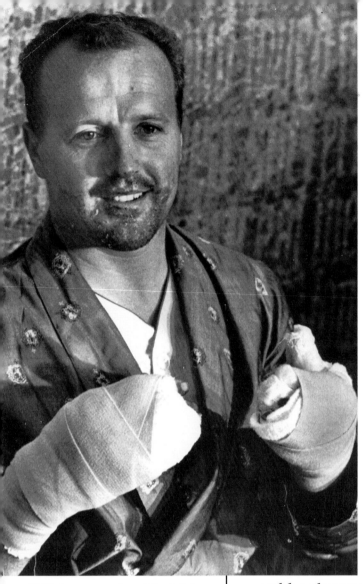

With burn marks still visible on his face, A. J. Foyt shows his bandaged hands to reporters and tells how he escaped death by leaping from his car after it hit a retaining wall and exploded. The race had taken place six days earlier, on June 4, 1966, in Milwaukee, Wisconsin.

ever. "You never know how good you can get a race car to feeling unless you try everything possible." Foyt tried everything and still the bad luck stretched on. He watched as Europeans Jimmy Clark and Graham Hill took the Indy 500 in 1965 and 1966, respectively. He watched as a young man named Mario Andretti captured the USAC championship for both years.

There were some who thought that Foyt was simply trying to do too much. "In the long run a team man will win more than an individualist," noted Richard Petty. "He feels he has to do it all by himself." Foyt ignored any criticism. "I only know one way to do things," he said. "My way."

In Milwaukee in 1966 Foyt was dealt his biggest dose of hard luck yet. During a practice run his suspension broke and he slammed into a wall. The collision ruptured a gas tank and the car burst into flames. "I knew I had to get out or just fry," said Foyt. "I gritted my teeth and put my hands in the burning fuel to raise myself out."

The flames scorched Foyt's hands, leaving severe burns. For weeks he was unable to even so much as go to the bathroom without the help of his wife. His record string of 82 straight races on the USAC championship trail ended. More significantly, as Foyt put it, "Suddenly I had all kinds of time to think about a lot of things I hadn't thought about before." All the close calls he had been in on the racetrack came back to him. Foyt wrote in his autobiography years later, "I realized there are some things I fear."

Doubts lingered as Foyt finally got back to racing. He managed to push them to the back of his mind by driving, as he said, "harder than I really wanted to. By pushing myself harder than I did before, I did start winning again, and that's the greatest therapy in the world."

At the beginning of the 1967 racing season, Foyt hired a new head mechanic. His name was A. J. Foyt, Sr. The younger Foyt realized that he had been trying to do too much. "My dad has joined our racing team and taken a lot of decision-making and detail work off my shoulders," Foyt said.

Others read even more importance into the move. Crew member Cecil Taylor, a longtime witness of Foyt's legendary, violent tantrums in the pits, observed that the elder Foyt "was the only guy I ever saw that could really deal with A. J." Not long after his dad became head mechanic, Foyt was raging at his crew about a subpar practice session. Tony put a stop to it by slamming his son against a wall and shouting, "What the hell's wrong with you, boy? You gone crazy?"

Father and son, as they had years before with A. J.'s first midget racer, worked together to build their own car for the 1967 Indy 500. The bright red Coyotes, as Foyt called them, could fly. For the first time in three years, A. J. felt confident about the race. "Now I feel we're ready," he said.

6

"IT'S MY TIME NOW"

At the 1967 Indianapolis 500, A. J. Foyt would have to beat a revolutionary turbo car piloted by Parnelli Jones. Though it ran smoother and weighed half as much as other racing engines, the turbine engine produced enough horsepower to blast Jones around the track at record speeds. Most of the drivers that year were cowed by Jones's new car. Foyt brashly predicted, "That car won't last half the race. Sooner or later the engine will overheat or the gearbox will go and it will be gone. No new car comes here and sorts itself out right away. Its time may come, but it's my time now. "

On race day, the turbo car glided out to an early lead. When heavy rain halted the action after only 18 laps, Jones led his closest pursuer by 12 seconds. Foyt's confidence held. Officials decided to resume the race the following day. "I'm so sure I'm gonna win this race," Foyt told

In 1967, Parnelli Jones brought a revolutionary turbo car to the Indianapolis 500.

47

Indianapolis Speedway owner Tony Hulman, "I ought to charge you for keeping my money overnight."

A dream visited Foyt that night. In the dream he led the race. Then, in the last lap, with the race all but won, he turned a corner into a calamitous multi-car pileup. Cars spun all over the track. Smoke and fire roiled. Foyt had no place to go but straight into the crash. The nightmare shook Foyt awake.

When the race restarted, Parnelli Jones doubled his 12-second lead by the 50-lap mark. A near crash with Lee Roy Yarbrough sent Jones onto the infield grass and allowed Dan Gurney to grab a brief lead. Jones deftly regained control of his car and simply coasted past Gurney back into first place. The high, whining engine sound of the turbo car seemed to mock all the roaring, laboring, piston-driven engines. The Indianapolis 500 began to resemble a bunch of pack mules in futile pursuit of a race horse.

"I had been certain he was going to break," said Foyt of Jones in the turbo car. "But when he got past the midway mark and kept going, I figured I was finished. All I could do was keep as much pressure on him as possible and hope for the best. But about the best I could do at that point was stay in the same lap with him."

The turbo car held everyone's attention. But Foyt, meanwhile, was running a brilliant race. As big a lead as Jones had on Foyt with 50 miles to go, Foyt had twice as big a lead on the next man. Foyt kept the pressure on Parnelli by "driving harder than I had ever driven." Finally, with but three laps to go, the turbo car crumbled under the strain. A six-dollar ball bearing failed, breaking the gearbox. Jones steered his pow-

erless car into the pits and Foyt took over.

With the race all but won, Foyt sped through the last turn. Then, without quite understanding why, he slowed his car to a crawl. "It was as though I had a premonition," he said. "I dreamed about it, and then I came around the corner and there it was." The nightmare crash had come true. Cars were spinning and crashing into the track walls. "If I hadn't already slowed down," said Foyt, "there was no way I could have gotten through it." Foyt tried to sneak through on the inside but quickly saw that there was no

Just as he had dreamed, Foyt (#14) turned the last corner of the 1967 Indianapolis 500 in the lead only to see a multi-car crash right in front of him. Foyt managed to weave through the debris and claim his victory.

hole. Then he cranked his car to the outside, calmly pumping his brakes, and squeezed past the disaster to a short stretch of open road and, said Foyt, "a beautiful checker waving at me."

It began to seem that there was nothing in racing that Foyt couldn't do. Stock car racing legend Junior Johnson said, "A. J. Foyt is the greatest driver that I ever knew. The best all-around. He could drive anything, anywhere, anytime. Won in about everything he ever sat down in."

It was important to Foyt to show the world that he could excel in every type of race there was. For that reason, just one week after his triumph at the Indianapolis 500, he set out for France to compete at LeMans, the biggest sports car race in the world, and one that no American had ever won before.

The race, a 24-hour marathon, teamed Foyt with Dan Gurney, a sports car specialist. Foyt quickly got the hang of the road course and during the race actually turned in faster lap times than his more experienced partner. He also had to pull a harrowing double shift at the wheel through the dangerous hours of foggy twilight before dawn. Gurney, it turned out, had known the perils of that particular shift and had made himself scarce when it was his turn to take the wheel. Foyt soldiered on, giving the impression that if he needed to he could have driven all 24 hours himself. When Gurney finally relieved him, Foyt had built an insurmountable lead. En route to victory, the Americans broke the course record by a wider margin than it had ever been broken before.

After making Europe's most prestigious race look like a vacationer's Sunday drive, Foyt came home to go after the USAC national championship. "Them sporty cars is all right," he said, "but, remember, I'm just a poor working boy who can't afford to race for fun." Foyt's head-to-head battle with two-time defending national champion Mario Andretti came down to the last race of the season, in Phoenix.

Holding a slight edge in the overall standings, Foyt needed only to finish near the top of the race to secure the championship. For a moment it looked like that would not happen. Avoiding a spin, Foyt careened off the track and was then speared by another out-of-control car. Andretti, leading the race, appeared a lock to take his third straight championship. But Foyt had worked out a deal with another driver named Roger McCluskey before the race. McCluskey zoomed into the pits and jumped from his car so that Foyt could finish the race and clinch the USAC crown. Mario Andretti ruefully observed, "Foyt will do anything to win."

The following year, on the same track, Foyt proved he would also do anything to help a fellow driver in danger. He sprinted from the pits into the aftermath of a three-car collision, pulling Johnny Rutherford from the flaming wreckage. Foyt ripped Rutherford's burning boots off, placed him on a stretcher, rode with him to the hospital, and stayed by his side all that day. "I'll never forget that, ever," said Rutherford, who would go on to win three Indy 500 races of his own.

Foyt knew that a race driver in trouble needed all the help he could get. Leading a 1972 dirt track race in DuQuoin, Illinois, by more than a lap, he pitted late to refuel. The fuel hose broke loose. "It hit me right in the head and my whole head caught on fire," Foyt recalled. "There wasn't a fireman around." He leapt from the cockpit and the left rear wheel of the driverless racer crushed his ankle and flipped him into the air. "I knew the infield had a lake in it, and so I'm trying to run for the lake, in a panic, and I'm limping on my ankle, like a horse with a broken leg, and my daddy was running after me with a fire extinguisher." Foyt, engulfed in flames, tripped on the guard rail and fell to the ground. "Dad came over the fence," said Foyt, "and saved my life."

That year Foyt made some noise on the stock car circuit. The biggest race held by NASCAR was the Daytona 500. Foyt served notice in 1971 that he was setting his sights on that race's checkered flag when he won pole position and battled Buddy Baker and Richard Petty for the lead for much of the race. A fuel problem kept him from winning that year but he came back in 1972 with a vengeance.

The 1972 Daytona 500 turned into a two-man race not long after the green flag came down. A. J. Foyt and Richard Petty dueled wheel to wheel at 160 miles an hour. Petty had already won the race three times. He would go on to win the Daytona 500 a record seven times, and would win over 200 NASCAR races in all. The record

A. J. Foyt drives Roger McCluskey's car after Foyt's car got wrecked. By finishing fourth in this 1967 race, Foyt won the USAC national championship.

books grandly proclaim King Richard, as he was known to his fans, to be the greatest stock car racer ever. But Foyt was pretty good himself. Bobby Unser once claimed, "Foyt's the best in a stock car I've ever seen."

The two living legends electrified the crowd for the first half of the race, swapping the lead 12 times in 200 miles. Foyt then started to forge inexorably ahead of his rival. Petty's car cracked just trying to keep up. He watched from the pits, his smoking, useless car nearby, as Foyt lapped the field. A triumphant Foyt, who had set a track record that would stand for eight years, exclaimed, "I especially like to beat the best in the big ones. When you beat Petty and the rest of the NASCAR racers, you know you're beating the best."

Back on Foyt's home turf, the feeling of disappointment mounted. At Indianapolis, it suddenly seemed to Foyt that everything that could go wrong would go wrong. In 1975 a desperate qualifying run—"I thrilled the hell out of myself a couple times out there," he said—gave Foyt pole position for the second straight year. He led the race for 47 laps and was within striking distance of the leaders late in the race when debris from a crash damaged his tires. A lengthy pit stop to remedy the problem dashed his chances. He finished third.

The following year, he came in second to Johnny Rutherford, who had gained the lead by running full-throttle for 23 seconds under the yellow caution flag and won the race when it was stopped due to rain after only 102 laps. "I feel sad for A. J.," said the winner of the shortest Indy 500 ever. "This is sort of a hollow victory, but I'll take it."

WELCOME TO FOYT'S HOUSE

After two near misses, A. J. Foyt wanted his fourth Indy 500 win more than ever. But the 42-year-old driver decided to approach the race differently than he ever had before. "I made up my mind I wasn't going to get keyed up," he said. "I just wasn't going to let the race bother me the way it has the last 20 years."

Foyt's calm, even-handed approach was put to the test during the practice runs. Old rival Mario Andretti edged Foyt in a much-hyped contest to become the first driver to circle the Speedway track averaging 200 miles per hour. Foyt stomached that defeat and also shrugged off a loss in the struggle for pole position to Tom Sneva. He had bigger victories in his sights. Race day, Foyt said, was "one of those days when I felt I was going to win from the start. I felt it with my steak and eggs that morning and I felt it as my challengers fell off, one by one."

A. J. Foyt won his third Indianapolis 500 in 1977. In 1991, CART ruled that no Indy Car could carry the number 14—unless Foyt himself was its driver.

With less than a hundred miles to go in the race, he had only one man left to beat. Foyt, trailing by nearly 40 seconds, started to make his move on Gordon Johncock, the defending USAC national champion. He jumped within striking distance by charging full-throttle for a few seconds under the yellow caution flag. Using the same trick that Johnny Rutherford had used to beat him the previous year was not below Foyt. He would do almost anything to win. Al Unser observed, "Foyt bends every rule in the book. He may even break a few. Hell, he rewrote the book himself. But we admire him for it. You've got to admire a man who knows how to win."

Foyt started turning in the fastest laps of the race at 190 miles per hour. Johncock saw his lead shrink to a mere four seconds. It seemed only a matter of time before Foyt blasted into first place in his blood red number 14 Coyote. Johncock's car, worked on by none other than Foyt's old mechanic/sparring partner George Bignotti, proved unequal to the challenge. With 15 laps remaining in the race a valve spring broke and Johncock's car crawled to a halt. Foyt roared on to become the first man in the 66-year history of the race to win four times.

People started to wonder when Foyt would announce his retirement, but A. J. was far from ready. "The hell of it is, if I didn't like the damn game and the challenge of it, I'd quit like everybody is yelling at me to do," he said. In 1979, for a record seventh time, Foyt won the USAC national championship. It seemed as if nothing could slow the aging racer down.

Four years later, in 1983, there finally came a day when Foyt did not want to race. He sat at the bedside of his sick father in a hospital room in Houston. Tony Foyt, who had been diagnosed with cancer, brought up the subject of a 24-hour sports car race being held at Daytona. "No use in you hangin' around here," he said. "Go on down there and run."

The marathon race became a labor of love for the younger Foyt. He had never driven a Porsche before, and he hadn't driven in a sports car race since his 1967 win at LeMans. But he grabbed the wheel of the unfamiliar car and, driving his heart out through fog and pouring rain, turned in faster lap times than anyone else in the race. After leading his team to victory, he let his teammates, two Frenchmen, split the first place money while he took the trophy back to his father in Houston.

In 1981, Foyt became the first person ever to win the Indianapolis 500 four times.

Tony Foyt died a few months later, but not before watching Foyt qualify for the Indy 500 for a record 26th straight time. Strangely enough, his mother had died two years earlier, also just after getting to see Foyt qualify. "They lived to see me make the race," said Foyt.

Foyt struggled after the death of his father. A friend of the family named Tim Delrose summed up an unusually close father-son relationship when he said of the two Foyts, "They fought with each other, they cussed each other, and they went everywhere together. They drove down all the roads. How many times do you see a thing like that between a father and a son?" Mechanic Cecil Taylor added, "Tony was not only his father, but probably his best friend, his mentor, his team and financial manager, just a whole lot of people rolled up into one."

According to the Foyt racing team manager, Sherby Blankenship, Foyt "just kind of wandered around in a fog for a year or two" after his Dad died. Cecil Taylor was on hand to see a gradual change come over the racer. "He's trying to reason things out, trying to take time to weigh things." When a wheel flew off of Foyt's car during a race at Phoenix, all the crew members braced themselves for a fearsome Foyt tantrum. Instead, the mellowing racer simply levied some constructive criticism, "like a gentleman," as Taylor said.

The burning desire to win at all costs had diminished. Foyt began to spend more time with his family. By the mid-eighties Foyt's family included grandchildren that, as one observer noted, could turn the once fearsome racing warrior "to Jell-O."

In 1985, the graying competitor entered America's oldest professional sports car race, the 12 Hours of Sebring. The grueling race served as a fitting punctuation mark for Foyt's growing status as a living legend. Only 31 out of the 78 cars that started the race were able to finish. Waiting until the end of the marathon to push his car to the limit, Foyt fended off a late charge by sports-car champion Derek Bell to win.

By the end of the decade, Foyt found himself competing against the children of rivals, like Mario Andretti's son Michael and Al Unser's son, Al, Jr. Racing's elder statesman began to reflect on the changing nature of his sport. "Before," he said, "you had to build a lot of your stuff, you had to put a lot of your time into it and come up with your own ideas, where now it's kind of like

NASA. You've got expert after expert, aerodynamics after aerodynamics. You've got so much
money behind the whole thing. Racing just ain't
the same anymore."

The days when one man could simply will himself to victory were over. Still, Foyt remained in
the thick of the action, a living reminder to a
tougher era of racing. To tangle with Foyt was
to prove your mettle on the race track. "You're
nobody," remarked 1986 Indianapolis 500 champion Bobby Rahal, "unless you've had a fist shak-
en at you by A. J. Foyt."

Even a brutal crash in 1990 at Elkhart Lake,
Illinois, couldn't get Foyt to quit. He begged doctors digging him from the wreckage to blot out
the pain by knocking him unconscious with a
hammer. Soon after the crash, which broke both
of his legs, Foyt hired the best rehabilitation
trainer he could find. Steve Watterson, who had
spent his career putting National Football League
players back together again, looked at Foyt's
injuries and said, "I've worked on some destroyed
joints, some compound fractures. But nothing
of this magnitude."

Foyt barked at Watterson throughout the dif-
ficult rehabilitation, "Fix my right foot so it will
go down! Don't worry about whether I can lift it.
In my game, if you lift your right foot, you lose."
A few months later, in May of 1991, with Foyt
ready to qualify for Indy for the 34th year in a
row, Watterson remarked, "I've worked with the
Olympics. Worked with the NFL. Known some
tough men... But never have I met anyone
tougher than A. J. Foyt."

Foyt dazzled the fans at Indy by qualifying for
the front row along with fellow racing legends
Rick Mears and Mario Andretti. He made the

Foyt was back at Indianapolis in 1994, not as a driver but as a team owner. Here he stands in a pit lane, timing his car driven by Bryan Herta.

race the next year as well, but in 1993 a stunned Indianapolis Motor Speedway crowd, gathered for the first day of qualifying, listened as Foyt proclaimed what was once unthinkable.

"Yeah, this is it," said Foyt into a microphone, his voice breaking. He told the crowd that a practice lap crash involving the driver of one of his cars had convinced him he needed to spend more time managing his racing team. Not quite able to hold back the sobs, he told the crowd that his days as a racer were over. "Let's face it, my years have passed on. It's a very sad day for me. This has been my life here."

A year later, in August of 1994, the Indianapolis Motor Speedway entered a new era by holding its first stock car race, the Brickyard 400. Sports car racers, short track specialists, Indy Car champions, as well as all of the top NASCAR drivers flocked to what would be the richest and best attended stock car race ever. Foyt could not resist. He was among over 80 racers vying for 43 spots in the race. When the dust from two whirlwind days of qualifying had settled, A. J. Foyt had put himself into the show.

"Welcome to Foyt's house," proclaimed a sign in the Indianapolis Motor Speedway stands on race day. He thrilled the crowd of over 300,000 by briefly shooting as high as second place. Mechanical troubles soon dashed his chances, but Foyt had shown, a few months shy of his 60th birthday, that he could still hang in there with the best of them.

STATISTICS

Indianapolis 500

Total Starts: 35

	Year	*Starting Position*	*Average MPH*
Wins			
	1961	7	139.130
	1964	5	147.350
	1967	4	151.207
	1977	4	161.331

Pole Positions

	Year	Average MPH
	1965	161.233
	1969	170.568
	1974	191.632
	1975	193.976

Career Statistics

Indy Car Wins:	67
Indy Car Pole Positions:	53
NASCAR Wins:	8
Sports Car Wins:	5
USAC National Championships:	7 ('60, '61, '63, '64, '67, '75, '79)
USAC Midget Car Wins:	22
USAC Sprint Car Wins:	27
USAC Stock Car Wins:	44
Total Major Events Won:	173

A. J. FOYT
A CHRONOLOGY

1935   Born Anthony Joseph Foyt, Jr., in Houston, Texas, on January 16

1953   Begins professional racing career at Houston area tracks

1955   Marries Lucy Zarr; begins racing sprint cars

1956   Son, Anthony Joseph III, is born

1957   Wins first USAC race, in Kansas City, Mo.

1958   Races in the Indianapolis 500; daughter, Terry, is born

1960   Wins USAC National Championship

1961   Wins Indianapolis 500; wins USAC National Championship

1962   Son, Jerry, is born

1963   Wins USAC National Championship

1964   Wins Indianapolis 500; wins Daytona Firecracker 400; breaks record for most career Indy Car wins; wins USAC National Championship

1966   Record streak of 82 consecutive Indy Car starts ends

1967   Hires father, Tony Foyt, as head mechanic; wins Indianapolis 500; wins, with Dan Gurney, the 24 Hours of LeMans; wins USAC National Championship

1972   Wins Daytona 500

1975   Wins USAC National Championship

1977   Wins Indianapolis 500

1979   Wins USAC National Championship

1985   Wins 12 Hours of Sebring sports car race

1991   Qualifies for first row at Indianapolis 500

1992   Races in 35th consecutive Indianapolis 500

1993   Announces retirement at Indianapolis Motor Speedway

1994   Races in inaugural Brickyard 400 stock car race

SUGGESTIONS FOR FURTHER READING

Engel, Lyle Kenyon. *The Incredible A. J. Foyt*. New York: Arco Publishing, 1970.

Foyt, A. J., and William Neely. *A. J.* New York: Times Books, 1983.

Golenbock, Peter. *American Zoom*. New York: Macmillan, 1993.

Higdon, Hal. *Finding the Groove*. New York: G. P. Putnam's Sons, 1973.

Johnson, Alan. *Driving in Competition*. New York: W. W. Norton and Co., 1971

Kleinfield, Sonny. *A Month at the Brickyard*. New York: Holt, Rinehart and Winston, 1977.

Libby, Bill. *Andretti*. New York: Grosset and Dunlap, 1970.

Libby, Bill. *Foyt*. New York: Hawthorn Books, Inc., 1974.

Petty, Richard, and Bill Libby. *King Richard: The Richard Petty Story*. New York: Doubleday, 1977.

Unser, Bobby, and Joe Scalzo. *The Bobby Unser Story*. New York: Doubleday, 1979.

Yates, Brock. *Sunday Driver*. New York: Fireside, 1990.

Magazines:

Moran, Malcolm. *Defying the Odds at Indy*. New York Times Magazine, May 25, 1986, p. 32.

Nack, William. *Twilight of a Titan*. Sports Illustrated, December 2, 1991, p. 67.

Ottum, Bob. *Get Out of the Way, Here Comes A. J.* Sports Illustrated, April 25, 1981, p. 99.

ABOUT THE AUTHOR

Josh Wilker has a degree in writing and literature from Johnson State College. He is the author of a biography of Julius Erving and a history of the Lenape Indian tribe for Chelsea House's Junior Library of American Indians series.

INDEX

PHOTO CREDITS: Bob Tronolone, Burbank, CA: pp. 2, 22, 32, 38, 46, 52, 54, 57; UPI/Bettmann: 25, 28, 30, 37, 49; *The Incredible A. J. Foyt,* Lyle Engle, Arco Publishing, New York, 1970: 8, 12, 16, 18, 21; Bruce Craig, Phillipsburg, NJ: 42; Reuters/Bettmann: 60.

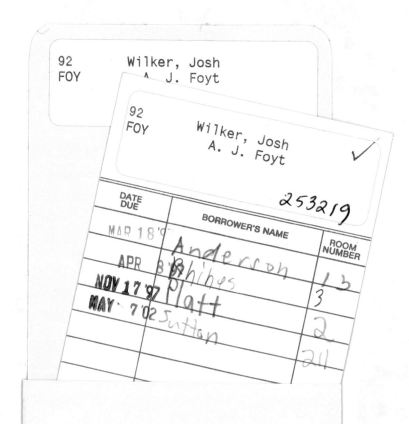

92
FOY
Wilker, Josh
A. J. Foyt

92
FOY
Wilker, Josh
A. J. Foyt ✓

253219

DATE DUE	BORROWER'S NAME	ROOM NUMBER
MAR 18 '97	Anderson	13
APR 8	Rhimes	3
NOV 17 '97	Platt	2
MAY 7 '02	Sutton	211